BENJAMIN BRITTEN

CANTICLE V

The Death of Saint Narcissus

for Tenor and Harp

Op. 89

Poem by T. S. Eliot

FABER *ff* MUSIC

In loving memory of William Plomer

Canticle V was first performed on 15 January 1975 at Schloss Elmau,
Upper Bavaria, by Peter Pears and Osian Ellis.

Duration approximately 7 minutes

Music © 1976 by Faber Music Ltd
First published in 1976 by Faber Music Limited
Bloomsbury House 74–77 Great Russell Street London WC1B 3DA
First amended impression 1996
Poem by T. S. Eliot reprinted by kind permission of the copyright owner
Mrs. Valerie Eliot, and Faber & Faber Ltd
Cover design by John Piper
Printed in Great Britain by Caligraving Ltd
All rights reserved

ISBN10: 0-571-50230-X
EAN13: 978-0-571-50230-1

The Death of Saint Narcissus

Come under the shadow of this gray rock –
Come in under the shadow of this gray rock,
And I will show you something different from either
Your shadow sprawling over the sand at daybreak, or
Your shadow leaping behind the fire against the red rock:
I will show you his bloody cloth and limbs
And the gray shadow on his lips.

He walked once between the sea and the high cliffs
When the wind made him aware of his limbs smoothly
        passing each other
And of his arms crossed over his breast.
When he walked over the meadows
He was stifled and soothed by his own rhythm.
By the river
His eyes were aware of the pointed corners of his eyes
And his hands aware of the pointed tips of his fingers.

Struck down by such knowledge
He could not live men's ways, but became a dancer before
        God
If he walked in city streets
He seemed to tread on faces, convulsive thighs and knees.
So he came out under the rock.

First he was sure that he had been a tree,
Twisting its branches among each other
And tangling its roots among each other.

Then he knew that he had been a fish
With slippery white belly held tight in his own fingers,
Writhing in his own clutch, his ancient beauty
Caught fast in the pink tips of his new beauty.

Then he had been a young girl
Caught in the woods by a drunken old man
Knowing at the end the taste of his own whiteness
The horror of his own smoothness,
And he felt drunken and old.

So he became a dancer to God.
Because his flesh was in love with the burning arrows
He danced on the hot sand
Until the arrows came.
As he embraced them his white skin surrendered itself to
        the redness of blood, and satisfied him.
Now he is green, dry and stained
With the shadow in his mouth.

T. S. Eliot (1888–1965)

from: Poems written in Early Youth (Faber & Faber 1967)

Canticle V
THE DEATH OF SAINT NARCISSUS

T. S. ELIOT

BENJAMIN BRITTEN
Op. 89

6

a dan-cer be-fore God

If he walked in ci-ty streets

He seemed to tread on fa-ces, con-vul-sive thighs and knees.

So he came out un-der the rock.

beau - ty Caught fast in the pink tips of his new_____

beau - ty.

Then he had been a young_____ girl

Caught in the woods by a drunk - en old man

13

rhythmic crotchets as before

So he be-came a dan-cer to God.   Be-cause his

flesh_____ was in love with the burn - ing ar - - rows_____

He danced_____ on the hot sand   Un -

- til the ar - - - rows   came.